March 2007

YES Lives in the Land of NO

Books by BJ Gallagher

A Peacock in the Land of Penguins
A Fable About Creativity and Courage
     with Warren H. Schmidt

What Would Buddha Do at Work?
101 Answers to Workplace Dilemmas
     with Franz Metcalf

Who Are "They" Anyway?
A Tale of Achieving Success at Work through Personal Accountability
     with Steve Ventura

Women's Work Is Never Done
Celebrating Everything Women Do

Everything I Need to Know I Learned from Other Women

Friends Are Everything

What's the Matter with Henry?
The True Tale of a Three-legged Cat
     with Cathy Conheim

Books by Steve Ventura

Start Right ... Stay Right
Every Employee's Straight-Talk Guide to Job Success

Walk Awhile in MY Shoes
Gut-Level, Real-World Messages Between Employees and Managers
     with Eric Harvey

Five Star Teamwork
How to Achieve Success ... Together
     with Michelle Correia Templin

Who Are "They" Anyway?
A Tale of Achieving Success at Work through Personal Accountability
     with BJ Gallagher

Forget for Success
Walking Away from Outdated, Counterproductive Beliefs and People Practices
     with Eric Harvey

Lives in the Land of **NO**
A Tale of Triumph over Negativity

BJ Gallagher
& Steve Ventura

Illustrations by Todd Graveline

BERRETT–KOEHLER PUBLISHERS, INC.
San Francisco
a BK Life book

Berrett-Koehler Publishers, Inc.
235 Montgomery Street, Suite 650
San Francisco, CA 94104-2916
Tel: (415) 288-0260
Fax: (415) 362-2512
www.bkconnection.com

Ordering Information
Quantity sales. Special discounts are available on quantity purchases by corporations, associations, and others. For details, contact the "Special Sales Department" at the Berrett-Koehler address above.

Individual sales. Berrett-Koehler publications are available through most bookstores. They can also be ordered directly from Berrett-Koehler: Tel: (800) 929-2929; Fax: (802) 864-7626; www.bkconnection.com

Orders for college textbook/course adoption use. Please contact Berrett-Koehler: Tel: (800) 929-2929; Fax: (802) 864-7626.

Orders by U.S. trade bookstores and wholesalers. Please contact Publishers Group West, 1700 Fourth Street, Berkeley, CA 94710. Tel: (510) 528-1444; Fax (510) 528-3444.

Berrett-Koehler and the BK logo are registered trademarks of Berrett-Koehler Publishers, Inc.

Printed in the United States of America

Berrett-Koehler books are printed on long-lasting acid-free paper. When it is available, we choose paper that has been manufactured by environmentally responsible processes. These may include using trees grown in sustainable forests, incorporating recycled paper, minimizing chlorine in bleaching, or recycling the energy produced at the paper mill.

Library of Congress Cataloging-in-Publication Data
Hateley, B.J. Gallagher (Barbara J. Gallagher), 1949-
  Yes lives in the land of no: a tale of triumph over negativity / by B.J. Gallagher & Steve Ventura.
    p. cm.
  ISBN 10: 1-57675-339-5; ISBN-13: 978-1-57675-339-2
  1. Optimism. 2. Success-Psychological aspects. I. Ventura, Steve. II. Title.

BF698.35.O57H38 2006
149'.5--dc22

First Edition
11 10 09 08 07 06   10 9 8 7 6 5 4 3 2 1

For Warren H. Schmidt,
our friend and colleague,
whose philosophy of life is
"to try again and succeed"

Contents

Preface   ix

Part I — The Parable   1

Part II — From Parable to Practice   97

    Is the Land of NO Familiar to You?   99

    Where to Begin ...   101

    Do You Work in the Land of NO?   103

    The Language of NO   106

    What Lies Behind the Language of NO?   108

    Some of the Many Reasons Why People Say NO   111

    Counter-Strategies for Turning NO into YES   113

    How Do You Know When NO Is Final?   121

    Is It Them . . . or Us?   123

    Mistakes We Make When Searching for YES   125

    What Do You Hear When Someone Says NO?   128

    Learning from NO   131

    A Case Study: Power of Positive Persistence   133

    Creating a World of YES Wherever You Are   137

    If You're a Manager or the Leader of a Group . . .   140

    How Do You Find Your Way Through the Land of NO?   143

Acknowledgments   145

About the Authors and the Illustrator ...   147

Information about Seminars, Keynotes, and Consulting   155

Dear to us are those who love us ...
but dearer are those who reject us as unworthy, for they add another life:
they build a heaven before us whereof we had not dreamed,
and thereby supply to us new powers out of the recesses of the spirit,
and urge us to new and unattempted performances.
— Ralph Waldo Emerson, essayist and poet,
in *Essays, Second Series*

Preface

It's no secret that we live in a world full of NOs. Seems like everywhere we turn, we're confronted by shaking heads, thumbs down, brick walls, brush-offs, closed doors, and, of course, the NO word itself. NOs surround us — in our workplaces, in our communities and places of worship, in government, in social settings, in schools, and even within our families. Some days we wonder, "Why bother?" Trying to find happiness and success in this endless landscape of negativity is just too hard, it seems.

But then we remember . . . there are also YESes out there among the many NOs. There are fewer YESes than NOs, to be sure, but usually all you need is one — the right one. Whether you're applying for a job, making a request, looking for a house, dating to find the right mate, seeking some type of approval, selling a product or an idea (or yourself), or trying to organize others into getting something accomplished, you're going to encounter many NOs. The challenge is: how do you persist and persevere in your quest for the YES that you know is out there somewhere?

We have good news for you: Help has arrived!

Think of this book as a personal travel guide for your journeys in the Land of NO. The first half is the tale of others' adventures with negativity — some successes, some failures, and lots of lessons learned along the way. The second half offers a collection of tips, strategies, quizzes, and tools to help you find your own way through the Land of NO — at work and in your personal life. Taken together, the two parts of this book provide a how-to manual that's both practical and entertaining. It will help you find the YESes you seek — faster, more effectively, and with a lot less discouragement and despair in the process.

Read it and reap . . . great results!

BJ Gallagher
Steve Ventura
March 2006

Part I

THE PARABLE

The Land of NO
is a discouraging place —
populated by frowns
and shrugs,
scowls and
furrowed brows.

Everyone is so solemn,
so somber,
so deadly serious,
you'd think they were expecting
the end of the world.

If you have an idea,
    Naysayers point out
        how "it will never work."

If you're looking for opportunity,
    doors are politely but firmly
        shut in your face.

If a project excites you,
    a wet blanket is promptly dispatched.

And heaven forbid
    you should dream of new possibilities!
There are more than enough
    Soldiers of Stagnation
        to trample your spirit.

Despite all that,
   I keep traveling to
     the Land of NO —
not because I love it so,
but because of what I learned some time ago:

The Land of NO
   is where YES lives.

YES?

Yes.

YES lives in the Land of NO.

"It is a most curious thing,"
     I've often thought
     and remarked to others,
"how YES resides
     with all his Negative Neighbors."

And it's definitely a challenge
     to find YES at all
in the midst of such
     Sorrowful Souls.

How strange,
   how odd,
         how perplexing,
and also
      how frustrating!

So what's a person to do —
a person like me
   in search of YES?

In the beginning,
my forays into the Land of NO
were dismal failures.

I bumbled and fumbled,
        wobbled and bobbled.
All those NOs really threw me.

My intentions were good,
        my idealism high,
but I was young,
        inexperienced,
                and naive.

When I encountered a NO,
    I'd get stopped in my tracks.

Sometimes I'd sulk,
    sometimes I'd seethe,
        and every once in a great while
        I even cried.

I wanted so desperately
to find a YES,
    but I hadn't a clue
    how to do that.

I looked around
and saw others
        making their way
        into the Land of NO.

"Maybe I should watch them
 and see how it's done,"
        I thought to myself.
"They obviously know something
 I don't know."

The first person I chose to watch
was my good friend N. Thusiasm.
He's a very excitable fellow
        who's often bubbling over
                with lots of good ideas.

I've always enjoyed
        his zest and his verve.

His energy was high
as he rushed into the Land of NO
     one day.

He didn't take much time
     to look around.
He just burst through
     the first doorway he came to.

Don Rock de'Boat looked up
from the pile of papers
on his desk.
"N. Thusiasm,
how are you today?"

N. Thusiasm couldn't contain himself.
He told Don all about
his idea
for a new kind of widget
he thought
the Land of NO should make.

Don Rock de'Boat listened politely
as N. Thusiasm rattled on,
     his pace racing
         and his pitch rising
             in intensity.

Finally he paused
    for breath,
and Don Rock de'Boat
    tried to rein him in:
"I appreciate your creativity,
    really I do,
        but our current product line
        is doing just fine.
"I don't see the need
    for this new widget you're proposing.

"Thanks for stopping by,
    but I have a ton of paperwork to do."

He nodded toward the door,
    indicating that N. Thusiasm
    should leave.

Poor N. Thusiasm.
His high hopes
        had been dashed.
I watched him as he left
Don Rock de'Boat's office,
        his head down,
        his shoulders slumped.

He was so disappointed.
        I could understand why.

Running into NO
        really brings you down
        with a thud.

Sometime later
I noticed someone else venturing into
        the Land of NO.

Wynot Now was his name.

I didn't know him well,
but I'd seen him around
        the Land of NO before.

I nodded hello
    as he passed me.

He smiled hello in return.
"Can't stop to chat," he said.
"I have something that needs approval
    right away."

"OK, catch you later,"
    I replied,
as he hurried on his way.

I watched
        as he knocked on a door
                and then went in.

May B. Later was on the phone,
and she motioned for him
        to hold on
while she finished
        her conversation.

When she hung up,
        he could see
        that she wasn't happy.
She seemed distressed
        and distracted
                by the phone call.

She tried to erase her frown
        as she turned her attention to
        Wynot Now.

"What's up?"
        she asked.

"I have the proposal
we discussed last week.
I've been working on it
with my team
ever since you and I talked,"
Wynot replied.
"It's ready for your signature."

"Oh my," she sighed,
      as the furrows
           in her brow deepened.

"You couldn't have come
      at a worse time.
You wouldn't believe
      the week I've had."

Wynot Now didn't know
what to say …

The two of them
just looked at each other
in silence.

"Just leave it here,"
        May B. Later finally said,
                extending her hand
                        to take the proposal.

"I'll get to it when I can."

Wynot handed it to her,
        but he had an awful feeling
                in the pit of his stomach.

"When should I expect
to hear back from you?"
        he asked.

"Not sure,"
        she replied.
"Like I said,
I'll get to it when I can."

Wynot Now knew better than to push.
He'd dealt with May B. Later before.

"Well, thanks for your time,"
        he muttered lamely
                as he headed out the door.

"Sure, no problem,"
        she said
                as she picked up her phone again.

Wynot Now closed the door carefully
behind him,
making sure
not to let it slam.

I saw the look on his face
as he passed me again.
I could see he was frustrated.

He didn't say a word,
but he didn't have to.

"Too bad," I thought to myself,
"I'm sure it was a good proposal."

I learned a few things
from the experiences
of N. Thusiasm
and Wynot Now.

But they weren't having
any more success
than I was.

I began to wonder . . .
"Maybe there *is* no YES
in the Land of NO,
after all.
Maybe I'm on
a futile quest,
along with everybody else."

I decided to watch more people
and see if they fared any better.

Ima Newheer's adventure
        was of a different sort.

She'd heard all about
the Land of NO
        before she ventured in.
She felt that her fresh perspective
        was just what the Land of NO needed.
She would transform
        this negative place
                in no time!

Eager to make her mark,
        she set to work
                right away,
formulating grand plans
        and creating a lofty vision
                for what she wanted to accomplish.

She worked hard to prepare
an impressive presentation
for the leadership team,
> B. A. Skeptic,
> Nomo Money,
> and Stan S. Quo.

She scheduled time
> on their calendars;
she booked a conference room;
> she worked on her Pow R. Point slides.

She took great pains
> to make sure that
> > she'd covered all her bases.

Her Big Day arrived,
and Ima Newheer did a great job,
        according to Nomo Money's assistant,
            ReNay Sayer,
                who also sat in on the meeting.

I've worked with ReNay
many times in the past,
        and I know
        she's not easily impressed.

But she told me later
        that Ima Newheer
            had made a good presentation.

Nevertheless,
the leadership team didn't go for it.

Stan S. Quo told her,
"I admire your imagination
and your ambition,
          but you're new . . .
you clearly don't understand
how things work here."

"Right," chimed in Nomo Money,
"and especially
        our financial planning process.

"What you're proposing
        is entirely too expensive.
What assurance do we have
        that our return on investment
                will be as high
                        as you suggest?"

B. A. Skeptic saw that
Ima Newheer was crestfallen.

He tried to be helpful:
"I'd suggest you spend
        some time here
                getting acclimated.

"Learn the ropes.
    You'll have better success
            if you work hard,
                    try to fit in,
        and learn how we do things here."

"Right," Nomo Money added,
"and learn how our financial systems work.

"You need to build a track record here
        before you can expect us
                to invest this kind of money."

Ima Newheer was speechless.

She thought she'd done everything right.
She figured that her track record
    in her previous land
        would count for something.

She was mistaken.

She stammered her thanks
        to the leadership team
and beat a hasty retreat
        to the ladies' room,
                fighting back her tears.

ReNay Sayer told me
    she felt sorry for Ima,
        but what could she do?

ReNay was just an assistant,
    after all.

I learned some useful things
from Ima Newheer's experience,
        just as I had from the others'.

I tried to analyze
what the NOs were about . . .

Were these problems of *principles*
        or of *personalities*?

I wasn't encouraged
by what I had seen thus far,
        but I wanted to learn from their failures,
        as well as my own.

I was still holding out hope
        that YES did, indeed,
                live in the Land of NO.

I determined to watch
a few more people
        to see what else
        I could pick up.

Sometimes it was painful
to watch others' experiences . . .

I recall the day
that Toolit L. Info
    had the misfortune
    of knocking on the door
        of Gimme Moredata.

I cringed as I watched . . .
anyone could have seen
    that disaster coming
        from a mile away!

Anyone except
    Toolit L. Info,
        that is.
For it's often the case
    that we can't see our situation
        because we're *in* it.

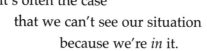

I tried to warn him,
       but he would not be deterred.

Poor guy,
       Toolit L. Info
       didn't stand a chance
              trying to get a YES
              from Gimme Moredata.

And I'll never forget the time that
Seymour Sales,
     who was in one department,
locked horns with Hugh Kant,
     in charge of another department.

Two dynamic personalities like that . . .
     the sparks flew!

Seymour Sales was a top producer
and accustomed to
getting what he wanted.

But Hugh Kant carefully guarded
his turf,
and when he heard
that Seymour
had been butting in,
making suggestions
for his department . . .

Hugh went ballistic!

Boy, I'd like to have been
       a fly on the wall
to see the clash of those two titans.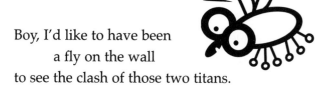

It must have been
       really something!

The tale of their encounter
was all over the Land of NO
        within hours.
The NO grapevine
        works faster than the Internet!

And I came to understand
    that the Land of NO
can be a significant problem
    even for powerful people.

Over time
  I had the opportunity
    to witness
many unhappy encounters
    in the Land of NO.

I learned
  there are myriad ways
    to go wrong . . .

but far fewer ways
  to go right.

Perhaps the saddest case
I ever saw
was Wy Trye —
a very nice guy,
quietly competent,
dependable,
and reliable.

I liked him a lot,
and we became friends
after a while.

He was a bit shy,
        so it took time
        to really get to know him.

But once I did,
I discovered that
        he had lots of good ideas.
However,
        he never shared them
                with anyone but me.

When I asked him why,
he said,
"Oh, no one's gonna listen
    to suggestions from me.
They'd just blow me off,
    I'm sure.

"It's best not to stick your neck out
    here in the Land of NO.
I'm OK with just doing my job,
    collecting a paycheck,
        and going home.

"My ideas
    probably aren't that good anyway,"
    he concluded.

There was no point
    arguing with him.
He'd made up his mind
    that he didn't want to risk rejection,
and he had long ago
    judged himself
        as not that smart.

He was a sad case,
    Wy Trye.

It appeared that
    the Land of NO
        existed right inside
            his own head!

Now you might think that,
after seeing
so much disappointment,
        frustration,
            and unhappiness
                in the Land of NO,
I'd have pulled up stakes
        and left for good.

"Who needs it?"
        you might ask.
"Why don't you just
  steer clear of that place
  altogether?

"Life's too short
        to deal with
            such negativity."

You'd be right,
        of course,
and that's just what many people do.
The Land of NO is so daunting,
        they never venture in at all.

And I might have done the same,
        except for one little detail . . .

Hope dies hard,
     and
I still had hope that
somewhere out there
     in the middle of all those NOs
          there lived a YES.

And that's what I was after . . .

     YES.

I didn't need
            lots of YESes,
                        after all . . .
In most cases
            just one will do —
                        the right one.

But I would never find it
if I weren't willing
            to travel through
            the Land of NO.

By now,
I was becoming
quite a good student
        of the Land of NO.

I made notes to myself
        on what didn't work.

I saw that, while many NOs were external,
others were internal . . .
        and sometimes
        a combination of both.

I'd learned a lot from failure,
 my own and others' —
and I certainly picked up
 plenty of tips
 on what *not* to do.

NO had been my teacher . . .

and if they ever offer
a degree in NO-ology,
 I'd certainly qualify
 for top honors!

But I still had a ways to go
　　　before I was ready
　　　　　to find my YES.

I needed to learn more about:
how to avoid some of those NOs,
how to turn them around
　　　if I couldn't avoid them,
and how to keep going in spite of them.

It's always easy to find
　　　those who are defeated
　　　　　in the Land of NO.
I needed to find
　　　those who were *winning*
　　　　　the YESes they pursued.

I had to keep looking
　　　and learning . . .

I broadened my search.

I discovered
Percy Verance diligently going
from door to door,
      determined not to quit
            until he found the YES
            he was seeking.

He'd teamed up with his close friend Téa Nacity,
who held on to her goals and dreams
      the way a bulldog
            grips a bone.

Her petite physique
      belied
            the strength of her spirit.

She was amazing!

Percy Verance and Téa Nacity
had figured out
    that together they had
    a better chance
    of finding YES
        than if they each took on
        the Land of NO alone.

Two heads really *are*
better than one,
    particularly if the two heads
        are theirs.

Then they told me about
someone else I should meet —
        good old Wilby Patient.

He was staying the course,
        enduring one NO after another,
quietly confident
        that his YES
                was out there
                        somewhere.

Figuring that he had time on his side,
        Wilby Patient taught me that
                victory is sometimes
                just a matter of
                outlasting the NOs.

It did my heart good
when Wilby Patient finally
won the day.

And, of course,
everyone in the Land of NO
          still talks about
how Addie Tude
actually managed
to transform
          several very stuffy NOs
                    into enthusiastic YESes.

She greeted their rejection
with good humor and grace.
          When they said "NO,"
          what she heard was "Not yet."

It was remarkable
          how she listened
                    through such a positive filter.

She bowled people over
          with her charm and persuasiveness.

(And I wondered
        if I should introduce her
                to Wy Trye . . .)

But the highlight of my education
in the Land of NO
        began the day I happened to join
        a group of folks who were having lunch.

The place was crowded
        and there was nowhere else to sit.

"May I join you?"
        I asked.

"Sure, pull up a chair,"
        one of them invited.

They introduced themselves
and made me feel welcome.

"I'm Bea Prepared,"
        the first one said.

"Hi, I'm F. Forte,
 and this is my friend Werk Hardt,"
        the second one said.

"And I'm Will Ingness,"
        the third one said,
        extending his hand
        to shake mine.

"My name is F. Lex Ability,"
        another chimed in,
"and sitting next to me is Goode Tyming."

"Glad to meet you all,"
        I replied,
        as I dug into my lunch.
"Please,
        don't let me interrupt."

They smiled at me
        and resumed their conversation.

They were all excited
about their quest for YES,
and by the end of our lunch,
they had invited me to join them.

"What great people,"
          I thought,
"and such a worthy cause . . ."

     It made me feel good
          to be part of such
                    a positive endeavor.

The project we launched
took many months of traveling
through the Land of NO.

Sometimes we traveled together,
when we had
a particularly tough NO to tackle.

Other times we traveled individually,
        scouting the terrain,
        gathering information,
        securing resources,
        enrolling support,
        and assessing barriers.

But whether alone or together,
        the going was never easy.

I can't tell you the number of NOs
we had to deal with along the way . . .

No sooner had we started our project
than we ran smack into Lotta Fear,
who tried her best to dissuade us
from our quest.

Then we encountered I. M. Swamped,
who claimed he was far too busy
to consider anything new.

We had to chuckle
when we had coffee with R. U. Nutz,
who rolled his eyes
when we told him of our plans.

He didn't say NO
in so many words,
but we could tell that
he thought
we'd taken leave
of our senses.

Then there was the day
I went to meet with
the evil twins
Ben There and Don That ...

while the rest of our group
was trying to handle
myriad objections
from Yeah Butts.

We reconvened later on
to compare notes,
>   and to prepare
>   for our meeting
>> with the toughest of characters,
>> Noway Jose,
>> and his annoying assistant,
>> Red Taype.

It took all of our skills,
>   our patience,
>> and our charm
to deal with that pair!

I can tell you,
there were days when we wondered
        if we'd ever find our YES . . .

And I must admit,
        there were times I thought
                about quitting the team.

"Yes, it's a noble cause,"
        I thought to myself,
"but sometimes
 all the negativity
 is just too much."

I'm only human, after all.

And I began to understand
        why even the best of optimists
                sometimes give up.

But at those times,
when things were at their worst —
        and our project doomed to failure —
somehow,
        someone in our group
would win a small YES,
        and it was just enough
                to keep the rest of us going.

It helped that others joined us
along the way . . .

Percy Verance and Téa Nacity,
        impressed with our cause,
agreed to consult with us
        on a pro bono basis.

Wilby Patient helped us
        with our long-term strategy.

And Addie Tude facilitated
some of our meetings,
        brightening our spirits
        with her infectious energy.

Seymour Sales,
who always loved a new challenge,
stopped bugging Hugh Kant
long enough to give us a hand
in "selling" our project
to important people.

All in all,
it was one of the best experiences
        of my life.

I took everything I had learned
from my early failures
in the Land of NO —
        as well as what I had gleaned
        watching others fail, too —
                and put every one
                of those hard-earned lessons to use.

Then I let myself be inspired by,
and instructed by,
all the positive people
I'd met along the way.

Both Failure and Success
had been my teachers,
and I mastered their instructions well.

Did I discover some "secret"
to finding YES in the Land of NO?

Not really.

The "secrets" of success
are all "hidden" in plain sight —
        if only we will open our eyes to see
                and our minds to learn.

The "magic formula"
for finding YES in the Land of NO
is simple:
>Just watch and listen to
>those around you
>who are already finding their YESes.

If you want what they have,
>do what they do.

For they know
>the power of positive *doing*.

Finding YES in the Land of NO
is simple —
      but not easy.

If it were easy,
      everyone would do it.

But if you have what it takes —

        passion for what you want,
        willingness to risk rejection,
        courage to face the unknown,
        and
        commitment to stay the course —

then the Land of NO is the perfect place to be.

That is where
you'll find your YES.

THE END

FROM PARABLE TO PRACTICE

I took rejection and turned it into direction.
— Sally Jessy Raphael, radio and TV talk show host

Is the Land of NO Familiar to You?

- **Did you recognize any of the characters in the story?**
- **Were the people, situations, and struggles familiar?**
- **More important, did you see *yourself* in the story — have you traveled in the Land of NO?**

If yes, then you'll definitely want to read on . . .

What follows is a personal tool kit that will help you to reflect on the parable and apply its key lessons. You'll examine how you respond to negativity in your work and in your life. You'll learn strategies and techniques — not only for turning NOs into YESes, but also for *preventing* NOs in the first place.

You'll also be encouraged to reflect on (and change) your own negative thinking and reactions to others' ideas. Turning NOs into YESes is, after all, very much an *inside job.*

Dealing with NOs while you search for YES is a life-long challenge. There are always more NOs waiting in the wings. But the YESes are out there, too, if you're willing to do the legwork to find them. This next section will show you how to do just that.

Fortunate is the person who has developed the self-control to steer a straight course toward his objective in life, without being swayed from his purpose by either commendation or condemnation.

— Napoleon Hill, author of *Think and Grow Rich*

Where to Begin . . .

There are two places to look when trying to understand and improve your own encounters with negativity:

External Issues

NOs can result from a number of factors: competing priorities, others' desire to avoid change, group norms and culture, red tape and bureaucracy, financial contingencies, difficult personalities, and politics, among others. All these are problems in your environment and with *other* people.

Internal Issues

NOs can also result from your own negative thinking, as well as your failure to prepare, present, and persist in pursuit of what's important to you. These are self-inflicted problems within *you*.

The following pages examine external factors first; then we'll shift our focus to internal factors. Looking at both is essential for finding YES in the Land of NO.

Beware of allowing a tactless word, a rebuttal, a rejection to obliterate the whole sky.

— Anaïs Nin, French-born diarist and author

Do You Work in the Land of NO?

Read each of the statements below and decide whether it describes your working environment.

YES	NO	
___	___	1. New ideas are welcomed and appreciated where I work.
___	___	2. Taking initiative to improve things is an important part of our organization's culture.
___	___	3. Most of the time, it's easy to get ideas and suggestions approved where I work.
___	___	4. Questioning the status quo is encouraged at all levels in our organization.
___	___	5. Trying new things, launching pilot projects, and conducting experiments are all part of how we operate on a regular basis.
___	___	6. Risk taking is typically encouraged. A certain amount of failure is accepted as a part of how we grow, individually and collectively.
___	___	7. Most everyone where I work operates by the unwritten motto "Find a way to say YES."
___	___	8. Leaders set the tone for the organization — seeking input from all levels, giving new ideas fair and timely consideration, while keeping red tape to a minimum.
___	___	9. Coworkers and teammates are usually open to one another's suggestions and ideas.
___	___	10. Organizational policies and procedures are flexible to allow for exceptions and are changed when they impede innovation.
___	___	**TOTALS**

Scoring

If you answered YES to all ten statements, congratulations! You're very fortunate. You *don't* work in the Land of NO.

The more NOs you indicated, the more negativity in your workplace — and the harder you'll have to work to find a YES for your projects, ideas, and proposals.

If you answered NO to one to three statements, your organization is a pretty positive place to work. You have just a little bit of negativity to deal with.

If you answered NO to four to six statements, your workplace is a mixed bag — some negative elements counterbalanced by some positive elements.

If you answered NO to seven to ten statements, it's pretty hard to find much to be positive about — negativity dominates your corporate culture. You *definitely* work in the Land of NO. Tips and strategies on the following pages will be especially helpful to you. Take heart and read on . . .

We keep going back, stronger, not weaker,
because we will not allow rejection to beat us down.
It will only strengthen our resolve.
To be successful there is no other way.
— Earl G. Graves, businessman, entrepreneur, activist,
and publisher of *Black Enterprise* magazine

The Language of NO

Every group, every community, every organization has its own vocabulary and language. The Land of NO is no exception. Here are some common expressions of negativity. Which ones do you encounter in your daily life?

"That will never work."

"We've tried that before."

"They'll never let us do that."

"Now is not the time."

"Let's think about it for a while."

"It's too risky."

"We can't do that."

"It will be too much work."

"There must be a reason why no one has done it before."

"What evidence do you have that it will work?"

"There must be an easier way."

"We're too busy."

"It'll never fly."

"It's not my job."

"That's not the way we do things here."

"We have other priorities."

"That's great, but who's going do it?"

"Let's table it for now."

"Sorry, no budget for it."

"It's not my fault . . ."

"That's not exactly what I had in mind."

"The last person who tried something like that . . ."

"I like my idea much better."

"Maybe next year."

"Yeah, but . . ."

"No way."

And there are nonverbal NOs, like rolling the eyes, sighing heavily, tapping fingers on the desk, looking at a watch, frowning, scowling, looking exasperated, and so on.

Which of these many negative expressions do you encounter most frequently?

What Lies Behind
the Language of NO?

NO doesn't come from nowhere. It comes from feelings and perceptions, both real and imagined. Understanding what's *behind* a NO can help you begin to turn it around.

Fear

- Fear of the unknown and of leaving comfort zones; upsetting one's sense of balance (natural resistance to change).
- Fear of taking risks (potential negative consequences if things go wrong).
- Fear of change.
- Fear of losing one's job or of looking bad.
- Fear of speaking up, saying, "I don't know."
- *Many* other fears as well.

Experience

- New possibilities are filtered through negative past experiences.
- "We've tried that before, and it didn't work" syndrome.
- "No news is good news" — why change things when everything is fine?

Ego

- Not wanting someone with a good/different idea to look better than you.
- "Not invented here" syndrome.

Laziness

- New ideas/strategies typically involve more work, at least at first.

- Protecting/maintaining the status quo is perceived as requiring less work and effort.

Habit and Comfort Zone

- It's always easier to say NO.

- Who wants to get out of their comfort zone?

- Old habits can be very hard to break.

- "This is the way we've always done it."

Limited Resources and Competing Priorities

- Not enough time, money, or staff.

- Other projects seem more important.

Politics

- Personal agendas, sacred cows, and favoritism (among other things).

- Power struggles, egos, and issues of control all play a part.

Eighty-five percent of our customers say "no" at least once before buying.
— Ross Perot, Dallas billionaire and founder of Electronic Data Systems

Some of the Many Reasons Why People Say NO

NO perceived need

NO perceived benefits

NO clear understanding

NO time or resources to "experiment"

NO involvement in the idea

NO credibility for the person with the idea

NO history of success for similar ideas

NO perceived flexibility

NO perceived freedom to fail

NO authority on the part of the decision maker

What are some other reasons you can think of?

_____

_____

_____

Pick the top three reasons for NO that you encounter most frequently, and mark them with an X. As you read on, you can strategize about ways to start shifting some of those NOs into YESes.

Energy and persistence conquer all things.
— Benjamin Franklin, statesman, philosopher,
inventor, printer, and musician

Counter-Strategies for Turning NO into YES

NO perceived need:

Some people will not share your sense that a problem or issue (or opportunity) exists. As a result, they will see no reason to take on, and deal with, the discomfort of change.

Counter-strategy:

Sell the problem before the solution. Do your homework: collect the facts, crunch the numbers, and focus on specifics that will build the case that an intervention is warranted. Involve the person in identifying the downsides of inaction. Then propose your idea, explaining how it addresses those downsides.

NO perceived benefits:

Some people will not immediately see how your idea will benefit them or the organization. The value of your recommendation may not be apparent.

Counter-strategy:

Promote the pluses. Whenever you present an idea or recommendation to someone, include (and complete) the following: "And here's how this will benefit our group, our team, our organization, and you . . ."

NO clear understanding:

Some people will just plain not understand what you are saying or proposing. They may lack knowledge about, or experience in, the area you're addressing. And they may be unfamiliar with technical terms or specialized jargon that you use.

Counter-strategy:

Use simple, nontechnical language. Present the information in a manner they can easily understand. Periodically check for rapport ("Is this making sense?" or "See where I'm going with this?"). Invite questions. Close with a summary. When presenting your ideas, remember that *if they don't get it, you won't get it!*

NO time to "experiment:"

The people to whom you present an idea may be struggling with a heavy workload, competing priorities, and shrinking resources. As a result, they may perceive your recommendation as additional work . . . a drain ... a hindrance that they're not interested in tackling.

Counter-strategy:

Come prepared to address such concerns. State your willingness to take on the lion's share of work and responsibility. Offer well-thought-out suggestions on how necessary resources might be acquired. Describe how the potential gains outweigh the possible liabilities. And identify any past "experiments" that have resulted in major benefits.

NO involvement in the idea:

People will support that which they help create, and the opposite is also true. Some people will reject good ideas and plans coming from someone else merely because they weren't given the chance to add "their two cents." Others may feel that their interests have not been considered. Feeling left out typically leads to closed-mindedness.

Counter-strategy:

Solicit others' thoughts, opinions, and recommendations. When presenting an idea to someone, ask him or her for feedback and upgrade suggestions ("What would you do differently?" or "How can this be better?"), and act on what you hear. Look for opportunities to involve colleagues in brainstorming, planning, and implementation. Do your homework and present well-developed ideas, and make sure that you leave enough room for others to participate and develop some sense of co-ownership.

NO credibility for the person with the idea:

Due to factors such as limited experience or a low rank within the group or organization, you may lack credibility with those to whom you are presenting your idea. As a result, you will receive minimal or no serious consideration.

Counter-strategy:

Make sure that your presentation is thorough and well organized. Then solicit the help and support of someone who does have credibility with your target audience. Sell that person on your idea, and then ask him or her to "sponsor" your presentation and assist in the delivery. Or, you might want to ask for a mentor in the process. Individuals often respond positively to being asked to show someone the ropes, and they can help ensure that your presentation and/or project is successful.

NO history of success for similar ideas:

One of two situations is taking place: (1) ideas similar to yours have been tried in the past and produced poor results — no one wants a repeat experience; or (2) nothing like your idea has ever been proposed before — therefore, people conclude that it's either not necessary or too risky.

Counter-strategy:

If you're facing situation #1, be prepared to discuss why past endeavors failed, and what key learning can be applied to enhance the success potential of your idea. If it's situation #2, focus on the merits of your idea and the benefits to be gained. Discuss the risks of inaction (maintaining the status quo) and suggest that innovation almost always comes from "things we've never done before."

NO perceived flexibility:

Most people are leery of committing to any idea or proposal that they perceive as being set in stone — especially if that idea is new and untried. The fear of being saddled with a loser is a major factor leading to idea rejection.

Counter-strategy:

Build flexibility into your proposal. Suggest a small pilot project. Include provisions for monitoring, evaluation, and improving along the way. And make sure your design includes a "Plan B" in the event that things don't turn out well.

NO perceived freedom to fail:

This is a tough one! Often, people operating in risk-averse environments become so fearful of failure that they close their minds to innovation and new ideas. NO becomes an automatic, knee-jerk response to any idea that isn't, on face value, a sure thing. Selling your proposal to someone in this group can be a tough uphill battle.

Counter-strategy:

Focus on the costs of the problem and the benefits to be gained from your idea. Emphasize that *inaction* is, in fact, riskier than your proposal. Don't expect to get an approval or commitment in the first discussion. You're planting seeds here. Plan and schedule follow-up discussions. Focus on the natural leaders in the group and build critical support with them; don't waste your energy on the skeptics and cynics. Send copies of publication articles, statistical reports, and anecdotal evidence to the person(s) you're trying to influence. Research and share successes of other groups or organizations that have adopted similar approaches.

NO authority on the part of the decision maker:

Sometimes the person we approach for approval is not the right person to ask. He or she may even want to say YES but can't because it's beyond his or her scope of authority.

Counter-strategy:

Even if this person doesn't have the authority to give you what you want, it's a good idea to get his or her support anyway. The more buy-in you get from others, the more it helps your cause. Then ask the person for advice on who does have the authority to give you the YES you seek.

It's not personal ... it's just business.
— Michael Corleone, in *The Godfather*

How Do You Know When NO Is Final?

Finding YES in the Land of NO doesn't mean that every rejection can be changed. Sometimes NO is the right answer. Sometimes NO is final.

How do you know when to accept NO and move on, with grace and good humor?

We wish there were a simple rule for knowing when it's best to accept NO. Sometimes it's a gut feeling — you just sense that the NO is not open to negotiation or compromise. Other times, you do a mental calculus, weighing pros and cons, and you see that YES clearly is not going to happen. And sometimes it's a fatigue factor — you don't have the energy to try to get beyond NO.

Don't be discouraged. Not every NO can be turned into YES. What counts is that you stay in the game and go for the YESes that are really important to you. Sometimes wisdom means knowing when to go to bat and when to sit this one out.

NO is not failure. NO is not an indictment. Sometimes NO is just NO.

The first step on the way to victory is to recognize the enemy.
— Corrie ten Boom, Dutch author of *The Hiding Place*

Is It Them . . . or Us?

Pogo, the cartoon character drawn by Walt Kelly, famously said, "We have met the enemy and he is us." It is painful to discover that sometimes the reason we get NO from others has less to do with *them* than it does with *us*! Much to our consternation, we find that we frequently get in our own way in our quest for YES.

So let's turn our attention from others and focus on ourselves. Let's look at how we can improve our ability to maximize our chances of finding YES sooner and easier. The following pages provide an opportunity for self-awareness and learning how we can become more skillful at negotiating NO and more effective at finding YES.

When you make a mistake or get ridiculed or rejected,
look at mistakes as learning experiences,
and ridicule as ignorance.
Look at rejection as part of one performance,
not as a turn down of the performer.
— Denis Waitley, inspirational speaker and author
of *The Psychology of Winning*

Mistakes We Make When
Searching for YES

In our parable, we saw how several characters set themselves up for a NO response. Think back on the story and recall how reasons for rejection were internal, not external. Here are some common ways we sometimes sabotage our own success and walk right into a NO . . . listed with suggested remedies.

N. Thusiasm's mistake: *Acting too impulsively.* In our excitement, we want to jump right in without considering all the factors.

Remedy: *Take time to think things through.* Manage your enthusiasm appropriately, so that it isn't off-putting to others. Perhaps ask a trusted friend to help keep you from acting brashly.

Toolit L. Info's mistake: *Failing to do our homework.* We don't ask enough questions, do enough research, or get enough data to win a YES.

Remedy: *Make sure you've got all the relevant facts.* Due diligence will help prevent you from making ill-informed mistakes.

Wynot Now's mistake: *Bad timing.* We bring up our request, idea, or project at the wrong time and/or in the wrong setting.

Remedy: *Timing is everything.* Carefully choose the appropriate time and place to go for YES.

Seymour Sales' mistake: *Not enlisting the support of others.* Often there are key players whose support can determine the approval or rejection of something we want to accomplish, but we fail to get their buy-in early on.

Remedy: *Success is a team sport.* Don't try to go it alone. There is strength in numbers. Build alliances.

Ima Newheer's mistake: *Not having enough trust, credibility, or respect with others.* We make it harder for people to say YES if we don't have a track record that inspires their confidence in us.

Remedy: *Build a track record of good results.* When your work speaks for itself, your quest for YES will get easier.

Wy Trye's mistake: *Giving up too soon.* We overreact to a NO and give up in despair. We give it one good try and then bail out when the first try isn't successful. Or, we let past NOs deter us from ever trying again; we give up on ourselves completely.

Remedy: *Don't give up before the game is over.* Sometimes success is simply a matter of outlasting the resistance.

Other Common Mistakes

Mistake: *Rejecting input from others.* Sometimes we ask others for their suggestions and support but then reject their feedback if it doesn't fit with our ideas.

Remedy: *Don't ask for advice and help if you don't really want it.* Keep an open mind, especially with those who disagree with you. You can learn a lot by considering alternative points of view.

Mistake: *Seeking YES from the wrong person.* We approach someone who doesn't have the authority to say YES.

Remedy: *Know your audience.* Learn who the key decision makers are. Build relationships with people who can help you secure YESes.

Watch and learn from others' mistakes. Avoid making those same mistakes yourself. Finding YES in the Land of NO does not involve a mysterious process or some magic formula. There are mistakes you can avoid and skills you can develop to find more YESes.

Watch and learn from others' successes, too. Pay attention to people who seem to be good at finding their way to YES. Emulate their habits, traits, and strategies. Pay attention not only to what they're *doing*, but also to *who they're being*. People who work with integrity, honesty, and openness usually find more YESes than others.

What Do You Hear
When Someone Says NO?

What we hear when someone says NO is largely a function of who *we* are, rather than the NO itself. Our level of self-esteem, confidence, and optimism or pessimism colors how we hear and interpret NO from others.

Some people hear:

"You're stupid. Why on earth did you bring this to me?"

"What were you thinking?"

"You're a loser."

"I don't like you."

"You'll never amount to anything in this organization."

"Who do you think you are?"

"If I want you to have good ideas, I'll give them to you!"

These people personalize every NO, interpreting rejection as a sign of personal incompetence, stupidity, and sometimes even worthlessness. They suffer greatly in the face of NO and are not inclined to persist, risking yet more rejection and potential humiliation.

Other people hear:

"Not now. Ask again another time."

"It doesn't fit with my priorities or the organization's plans."

"I'm the wrong person to ask."

"This would mean more work for me. Make it easier."

"I'm not sold yet. Bring me more convincing data."

"It's too expensive. See if you can bring the cost down and we'll talk."

"I won't sign on until I know my boss would like it."

"Tell me how it can make a difference."

These people encounter NO but hear different messages entirely, interpreting rejection as simply a temporary setback. They retreat and regroup in order to try again another day. They won't be deterred from their desired goal.

What do *you* hear when you encounter NO?

_____

_____

_____

_____

You are not afraid of rejection.
You are afraid of what you believe will happen if you are rejected.
Identify the roots of that fear.

— Azriela Jaffe, therapist, author

Learning from NO

While none of us like to be on the receiving end of NO, there are sometimes things to be learned from our negative encounters:

NO can teach us where others' boundaries and limits are.

NO can show us how to be more persuasive in making our case.

NO sometimes shows us where our blind spots are.

NO helps us to develop patience, tenacity, and character.

NO can make us reevaluate our own position.

NO can help us see others' points of view more clearly.

NO can show us where we might be wrong.

NO can be a clue that others are challenged, are stressed, and could use a bit more sensitivity from us.

NO sometimes mirrors our own fears and doubts.

NO teaches us to try another way, becoming more creative and resourceful.

NO can help make us develop thicker skin and not take things so personally.

NO can make the eventual YES more meaningful ... and sweeter!

NO can be a valuable teacher, if you're willing to learn from it. Sometimes it's good to be grateful to NO.

Don't be discouraged by a failure. It can be a positive experience. Failure is, in a sense, the highway to success, inasmuch as every discovery of what is false leads us to seek earnestly after what is true, and every fresh experience points out some form of error which we shall afterwards carefully avoid.

— John Keats, English Romantic poet

A Case Study:
Power of Positive Persistence

"The secret to Bob's success is that no one in his life ever told him the meaning of the word NO," our friend Margret told us recently. She was referring to his phenomenal track record in a highly competitive business. She attributed his amazing achievement to his ability to persist in the face of rebuffs, rejections, and red tape. Bob is simply relentless — *cheerfully* relentless.

What's his secret? The power of positive persistence. People like Bob know what they want and set high goals for themselves. They love to achieve. They get a kick out of getting things done. They delight in finding creative ways to go over, under, around, or through roadblocks. They take NO as a personal challenge and almost seem to thrive on rejection. We can learn a lot from people like Bob.

All NOs are not created equal. Some NOs are strong, while others are weak. It's important to use all your senses, and your intuition as well, to determine how weak or strong a particular NO is. Listen to the tone of voice. Pay attention to nonverbal cues, body language, facial expression. If it's a written NO, read carefully between the lines. What's not being said is often as important as what is being said.

Don't take it personally. Chances are, most of the NOs you encounter at work have nothing to do with *you*. NO can be a function of bureaucracy, policies and procedures, red tape, office politics, budget constraints, and many other factors that aren't personal. However, your effectiveness at negotiating through NOs to get to YES *is* personal — it's your personal mastery of persuasion, persistence, and patience that will determine how many YESes you can find.

Timing is everything. Actors and military leaders know that timing is everything. Sometimes we get a NO simply because our timing was bad. Waiting for the right moment to voice your request and/or propose your idea can make a huge difference in how fast you can find the YES you seek.

Know your audience. Do your homework. Learn everything you can about the person(s) from whom you're seeking a YES. What's important to them? What are their hot buttons? How can you pitch your appeal in a manner that will win points with them? Use everything you know about your audience to establish and build rapport. Speak to your target audience in *their* language.

A partial NO is a win. Getting a partial NO means that you also got a partial YES — and a partial YES is better than no YES at all! Sometimes the YES you seek comes in pieces, in increments. Take what you can get now and be happy. You can always come back and work for a complete YES.

Pick your battles carefully. Some YESes are more important than others. It's essential that you evaluate and prioritize your goals, objectives, projects, and ideas so that you choose which ones to pursue at full throttle and which to put on the back burner for now. Sometimes you'll want to go for small YESes first, building momentum for the

big one to come. Other times you may want to go for the big one and drop the little ones altogether. Reevaluate your priorities regularly and then proceed accordingly.

It's easier to ask for forgiveness than for permission. Sometimes it's better to seek YES *after the fact*. This is a risky strategy, but if something is extremely important to you, it can be worth the risk. If you suspect that NO is the answer you'll get, sometimes it's better not to ask the question. Instead, take action and inform others later . . . or wait for them to find out on their own. If someone gives you a hard time, be as contrite as you can: "Oh, I'm sorry. I didn't realize I needed approval to do that. It just made sense to me, so I took action. I'm so sorry. It'll never happen again." You'll most likely be forgiven — but don't use this strategy too often or it'll stop working.

Just don't give up trying to do what you really want to do.
Where there is love and inspiration, I don't think you can go wrong.
— Ella Fitzgerald, *jazz legend, known as*
the First Lady of Song

Creating a World of YES Wherever You Are

While we're each looking to find more YESes in the Land of NO where we live and work, we mustn't forget that others may be wanting a YES from us as well. How can each of us contribute to transforming the Land of NO into a World of YES? What can we do to find ways to say YES more often?

Look for what you like in people, places, situations, and ideas. For many of us, our natural inclination is to first notice what we *don't* like. It's simply a habit — and habits can be changed. Make it a point to actively look for what you like, both at work and at home. Say, "YES, I like that," more often.

Piggyback on other people's YESes. Instead of saying, "YES, but … ," learn to say, "YES, *and* here's how I can see that working," or "YES, and here's how I can help make that idea or project even better."

When you feel the urge to say NO to someone, stop yourself and take a break to reflect before you speak. What are your motives in wanting to say NO? What is getting in the way of your saying YES? Have a conversation with the person who's asking for YES and share your concerns; see if he or she can address your issues to help change your NO to YES.

Model the behaviors you seek from others. If you want them to do their homework before bringing an idea to you, do the same with them. If you want coworkers, family members, and friends to say YES to you, look for every opportunity to say YES to them. Remember that timeless law of reciprocity: what goes around comes around.

Be resourceful in finding ways to say YES. Don't hide behind policies or tradition to say, "NO, it can't be done," or "NO, we've never done that before." It's easy and safe to say NO; it takes courage to say YES. Be courageous. If someone has a good idea, help him or her make it happen.

Recognize others who are positive influences in the Land of NO. Tell them how much you admire and respect their can-do attitude. Express your appreciation for all the ways they say YES. Let them know how much you enjoy being around them and/or working with them.

Whether your Land of NO is at work, at home, in school, in personal relationships, or in your community, you can make a significant difference in lowering the level of negativity. Your YESes add up. Other YESes will join yours. YES is contagious; it feels good.

Start now — right where you are. Find more ways to say YES.

We must be the change we wish to see in the world.
— Mahatma Gandhi, advocate of nonviolent political change
who brought independence to India

If You're a Manager or the Leader of a Group . . .

If you're in a leadership or management position, you play an especially important role in creating a Culture of YES. People look to you for guidance and support, for inspiration and courage.

Start with yourself. If you find more ways to say YES, those in your group or team will, too. Be a positive role model — a living example of the success that comes from saying YES.

Make sure you're walking your talk when it comes to saying YES. Don't tell people that you welcome their suggestions and ideas, and then shoot down their ideas when they come to you. If you say you're open to change and new thinking, then be open.

Reward others in your team or organization who are positive influences in the Land of NO. Tell them how much you admire and respect their can-do attitude. Express your appreciation for all the ways they say YES. Let them know how much you appreciate their contributions to the success of the group. Reward them in every way you can — what gets rewarded is what gets done.

If you have to say NO, you have a responsibility to explain why, and then point out what they need to do to get a YES. Tell them what they can do to change their idea or their approach in order to secure a YES.

Make sure that policies and procedures are kept to a minimum, to prevent them from piling up and forming barriers to saying YES. See to it that policies are flexible enough to allow exceptions and bending of the rules when the situation warrants. Review policies and procedures on a regular basis. Encourage others to question and challenge policies that don't make sense to them. Welcome their input — it's hard to say YES if people are tied up in red tape.

Provide training for your group in how and why you want them to say YES. Teach them the skills they should have; give them the information they require to make informed YESes. Equip them with all the tools they need to feel confident in saying YES.

Make your leadership mantra "Find a way to say YES." Live it every day.

**There is always time to do everything that really matters:
if we do not have time to do something,
it is a sign that it does not matter.**
— Peter Block, consultant and author
of *The Answer to How Is Yes*

How Do You Find Your Way Through the Land of NO?

Persist in pursuing what's important.

Endure discomfort; struggle is part of the pursuit.

Rethink your strategy when you encounter NO.

Steadfastly hold true to your values and ethics.

Envision what success will look like.

Voice your intentions and keep your commitments.

Express gratitude for support from others.

Risk is essential in finding YES; be courageous.

Enjoy and celebrate every bit of progress toward YES.

Nothing in the world can take the place of Persistence.
Talent will not; nothing is more common
than unsuccessful men with talent.
Genius will not; unrewarded genius is almost a proverb.
Education will not; the world is full of educated derelicts.
Persistence and determination alone are omnipotent.
The slogan "Press On" has solved and always will solve
the problems of the human race.
— Calvin Coolidge, 30th U.S. president

Acknowledgments . . .Thanks to Those Who Say YES

Many people must say YES for a book to be successfully published. First, the authors must say YES to commit to the project. The editor and publisher must say YES to bring the book into reality. Copy editors, designers, artists, and production people must say YES to turn the manuscript into a bound volume. Sales and marketing people must say YES to bring the book to market; publicists must say YES to getting the word out and building some buzz. And readers must say the biggest YES of all if the book is to be successful.

We want to say "Thank you" to all the terrific folks at Berrett-Koehler who said YES to this book:

- Steve Piersanti, our editor and publisher, whose enthusiasm for our idea gave us the incentive to write.

- Johanna Vondeling, who was always available for thoughtful editorial advice.

- Dianne Platner and Rick Wilson, who skillfully handled design and production.

- Kristen Frantz, Ken Lupoff, Mike Crowley, Robin Donovan, Marina Cook, Tiffany Lee, Ian Bach, Maria Jesus Aguilo, and Catherine Lengronne, who are pulling out all the stops to stimulate book buyers to say YES, too.

- Jeevan Sivasubramaniam, who played a key role as point man in coordinating all aspects of publication.

- Gail Caldwell, Ginger Winters, Bob Liss, Molly Fenn, Kathy Slater, and Diane Blattner, for all they do for us.

Thanks also to our skilled copy editor, Elissa Rabellino, who made sure all our *t*'s were crossed and our *i*'s dotted . . . instead of crossed *i*'s and dotted *t*'s!

A very special thanks to Todd Graveline, our talented illustrator, who put faces on our characters, bringing our book to life. His creative style provided a light touch to what can be a heavy subject. It is a joy and delight to work with you, Todd!

We want to thank our manuscript reviewers as well — several of whom said "YES . . . and you might want to rewrite this part, add this, delete that, to make it even better." (You see, YES sometimes arrives accompanied by caveats and suggestions.) Thanks to our reviewers: Leslie Yerkes, Martha Lawrence, Ken Blanchard, Rula Razek, Marcia Daszko, Jane Haubrich Casperson, Joel Suzuki, Mark Annett, Warren Schmidt, and Joel Marks.

And thank you to Steve Chandler who inspired our title — "yes lives in the land of no." It's a phrase he used in a seminar that we attended many years ago and we thought it was a perfect title for the tale we wanted to tell.

Most important, we want to thank our families, whose encouragement and support give us a steady stream of loving YESes to keep us going. Thank you. We love you.

And finally, we thank the One whose Divine YES is the source of our imagination and creativity. We're humbly grateful.

About the Authors
and the Illustrator . . .

To say yes, you have to sweat and roll up your sleeves and plunge both hands into life up to the elbows. It is easy to say no, even if saying no means death.
— Jean Anouilh, French playwright, director, and producer

BJ Gallagher

BJ Gallagher's favorite word is YES. Childhood photos show her with a big smile and happy eyes, her face lit up in eager expectation. The whole world looked like Disneyland to her — full of adventures, surprises, and amazing experiences. That positive spirit persists in adulthood . . . her work as an author, speaker, and consultant provides her with endless opportunities to say YES to others.

BJ's first YES to writing books resulted in *A Peacock in the Land of Penguins,* her most successful to date (published in 19 languages worldwide). Readers said YES to her work, so she kept writing more business books, including *What Would Buddha Do at Work?* (Berrett-Koehler) and *Who Are "They" Anyway?* (Dearborn Trade Press).

In addition to writing, BJ also says YES to speaking engagements and training seminars, along with occasional consulting. Her clients include IBM, DaimlerChrysler, John Deere Credit Canada, the American Press Institute, Phoenix Newspapers Inc., the Atlanta Journal-Constitution, Chevron, Farm Credit Services of America, Raytheon, Southern California Edison, Planned Parenthood, the City of Santa Monica, the American Lung Association, Nissan, Volkswagen, and Kellogg, among others.

Before saying YES to starting her own business in 1991, BJ was the manager of training and development for the Los Angeles Times, where she was responsible for management development, team building, sales and customer service training, internal consulting and organizational development.

BJ's academic training at the University of Southern California culminated in a resounding YES as she earned Phi Beta Kappa honors with her BA in sociology, graduating summa cum laude. She continued her education, pursuing a PhD in social ethics. Ultimately, she said NO to her advanced degree, but she smiles and acknowledges that "learning is its own reward."

BJ says YES to her home state of California, where she happily runs her seminar and consulting business in Los Angeles.

You can contact her at FindingYES@aol.com or (323) 227-6205. Web site: www.yeslivesinthelandofno.com.

Do what you feel in your heart to be right
— for you'll be criticized anyway.
You'll be damned if you do, and damned if you don't.
— Eleanor Roosevelt, first lady, author,
diplomat and humanitarian

Steve Ventura

According to his mother, Steve Ventura is recognized and respected for writing stuff (author), drawing stuff (graphic "artiste"), talking about stuff (educator), and bookmaking (the legal kind: publishing). With 25 years of human resource development experience — as both a consultant *and* someone with a real job — 10 years in law enforcement, 27 years as a parent, and 30 years as a husband, this is an individual who knows NOs . . . and YESes too.

As a consultant and trainer, Steve has schlepped bags through airports across the country. Scores of notable organizations have said YES to his services (and NO to his expense reports), including AT&T, General Electric, Shell Oil Company, Allied Signal Aerospace, General Dynamics, Pacific Bell, AMD, Northwest Airlines, Texaco, Exxon, and Texas Utilities. His inflated yet entertaining résumé lists management, leadership, communication, customer service, and performance improvement as his areas of expertise.

Before saying YES to starting his own business in 2002, he was vice president of product development for the Walk the Talk® Company, in Dallas, Texas. Prior to that, he was manager of operations training for the Bay Area Rapid Transit District, in Northern California, and before that he served as a police officer for the City of Berkeley.

Steve stretched his college years as long as he could, eventually earning a bachelor's degree in art and mass communication from California State University,

Hayward, and a master's degree in public administration from the University of San Francisco. Despite numerous rejections by editors, he has still managed to publish articles in trade journals such as *Training, Training & Development*, and *Food & Service*. His previous books include *Walk Awhile in My Shoes* (more than 750,000 sold) and the popular handbook *Start Right ... Stay Right*. Steve has written, edited, and produced 18 other highly successful business publications.

Contact Steve in Dallas, Texas, at (972) 317-6380 or his e-mail: sven2ra@comcast.net.

The reasonable man adapts himself to the world; the unreasonable one persists in trying to adapt the world to himself. Therefore, all progress depends on the unreasonable man.
— George Bernard Shaw, Irish-born playwright, winner of the Nobel Prize for Literature

Todd Graveline

Never one to say NO to an incredibly fun and rewarding experience, Todd Graveline jumped at the chance to lend his illustration talents to *YES Lives in the Land of NO*. Although he's said YES to many an illustration project in the past, this book marks his debut in the world of book publishing.

It's been said that Todd picked up a crayon as a toddler and said YES to a lifetime of drawing and art. Over time, his tools have varied from marker and ink to spray paint and software — with no rhyme or reason for his current medium of choice.

After graduating in the 1980s from the Milwaukee Institute of Art & Design, Todd worked for several years in advertising and publishing. When his first child was born in 1989, he left the real working world for good and embraced the life of an entrepreneurial, stay-at-home art guy. In 1992, he and his wife formed G2 Creative Inc., a two-person home-based advertising agency that has permitted them to enjoy both career and life — and allowed Todd to pursue his illustration passion. Over the years, his simple, whimsical illustrations have graced the pages of numerous magazines and newpapers, including *Time*, *Newsweek*, *TV Guide*, *Prevention*, *The Washington Post*, the *Chicago Tribune*, *Psychology Today*, *Forbes*, *BusinessWeek*, *Utne Reader* and the *Los Angeles Times*. Several years ago, he created, illustrated, and self-produced a children's CD-ROM mathematics game called *Professor Lumpy*, which was positively reviewed in *Time*'s ON magazine (called "irresistible") and in *PC Magazine* ("animation and sound effects are first-rate").

Along with commercial illustration and design, Todd says YES to the finer side of art as well. He brings his illustrator's eye, an exceptional knowledge of pop culture, and a bizarre stream of consciousness to a wacky variety of edgy artwork. His works range from simple silkscreens to mixed-media acrylics.

Todd can be reached at (414) 774-6595 or by e-mail at toddgraveline@aol.com. To see more of his art, visit www.toddgraveline.com or www.g2creativeinc.com.

I've not failed. I've just found 10,000 ways that won't work.
— Thomas A. Edison, inventor of the lightbulb

Risk! Risk anything!
Care no more for the opinions of others, for those voices.
Do the hardest thing on earth for you.
Act for yourself. Face the truth.
— Katherine Mansfield, New Zealand–born author,
a master of the 20th-century English short story

Information about Seminars, Keynotes, and Consulting

For seminars, keynote speeches, and training materials on "Creating a Culture of YES in Your Organization," please contact

BJ GALLAGHER
Peacock Productions
701 Danforth Drive
Los Angeles, California 90065

Phone: (323) 227-6205
Fax: (323) 227-0705
E-mail: FindingYES@aol.com

www.yeslivesinthelandofno.com

About Berrett-Koehler Publishers

Berrett-Koehler is an independent publisher dedicated to an ambitious mission: Creating a World that Works for All.

We believe that to truly create a better world, action is needed at all levels — individual, organizational, and societal. At the individual level, our publications help people align their lives with their values and with their aspirations for a better world. At the organizational level, our publications promote progressive leadership and management practices, socially responsible approaches to business, and humane and effective organizations. At the societal level, our publications advance social and economic justice, shared prosperity, sustainability, and new solutions to national and global issues.

A major theme of our publications is "Opening Up New Space." They challenge conventional thinking, introduce new ideas, and foster positive change. Their common quest is changing the underlying beliefs, mindsets, and structures that keep generating the same cycles of problems, no matter who our leaders are or what improvement programs we adopt.

We strive to practice what we preach — to operate our publishing company in line with the ideas in our books. At the core of our approach is stewardship, which we define as a deep sense of responsibility to administer the company for the benefit of all of our "stakeholder" groups: authors, customers, employees, investors, service providers, and the communities and environment around us.

We are grateful to the thousands of readers, authors, and other friends of the company who consider themselves to be part of the "BK Community." We hope that you, too, will join us in our mission.

A BK Life Book

This book is part of our BK Life series. BK Life books change people's lives. They help individuals improve their lives in ways that are beneficial for the families, organizations, communities, nations, and world in which they live and work. To find out more, visit www.bk-life.com.

Be Connected

Visit Our Website — Go to www.bkconnection.com to read exclusive previews and excerpts of new books, find detailed information on all Berrett-Koehler titles and authors, browse subject-area libraries of books, and get special discounts.

Subscribe to Our Free E-Newsletter — Be the first to hear about new publications, special discount offers, exclusive articles, news about bestsellers, and more! Get on the list for our free e-newsletter by going to www.bkconnection.com.

Participate in the Discussion — To see what others are saying about our books and post your own thoughts, check out our blogs at www.bkblogs.com.

Get Quantity Discounts — Berrett-Koehler books are available at quantity discounts for orders of ten or more copies. Please call us toll-free at (800) 929-2929 or email us at bkp.orders@aidcvt.com.

Host a Reading Group — For tips on how to form and carry on a book reading group in your workplace or community, see our website at www.bkconnection.com.

Join the BK Community — Thousands of readers of our books have become part of the "BK Community" by participating in events featuring our authors, reviewing draft manuscripts of forthcoming books, spreading the word about their favorite books, and supporting our publishing program in other ways. If you would like to join the BK Community, please contact us at bkcommunity@bkpub.com.